IN MY FATHER'S HANDS2

Breaking the Soul Ties of Sexual Sin

IN MY FATHER'S HANDS 2

"They have healed the wound of my people lightly, saying, 'Peace, peace,' when there is no peace.

Jeremiah 8:11

IN MY FATHER'S HANDS 2

Copyright © 2025- Zanetta L. Collins

All rights reserved. No part of this book may be reproduced or transmitted in any form or by any means, electronic or mechanical, including photocopying, recording, or using any information storage and retrieval system without permission in writing from the publisher. All scripture quotations are taken from the HOLY BIBLE, NIV, NLT®, Copyright ©1973,1978,1984. Spiritual criminals, identified and arrested,

by Timothy Atunnise.

The Collins Christian Co.

IN MY FATHER'S HANDS 2

LCCN: 2025923900

Publication Date:

Printed in the United States of America.

ISBN- 979-8-90148-347-3

Editing: Arnetta Raines

Pagination: https:

Cover:

https://www.fiverr.com/zproartz Images:

Makeup:Zanetta L Collins

Hair: Zanetta L. Collins

DEDICATION

If you are tired of traveling around that same mountain as the Israelites did around Mount Seir, this book is for you! If you desire to learn and understand how the enemy works, not just naturally but spiritually, and how you, as a believer, can combat the tools of the enemy with the tools that God has given you to uproot *sexual sin* from your life! This book is dedicated to you!

ABOUT

Zanetta Lee Collins was born in Fort Ord, California, to Valerie and Luther Collins Jr. Her upbringing was marked by adversity. Yet, it became the foundation for her unshakable resilience and purpose. Faced with significant challenges early in life, Zanetta learned to draw strength from her trials, determined to break generational cycles and carve out a better future for herself. Athletics became her refuge—a safe space where she could channel pain into passion. Her talent and tenacity on the basketball court earned her a college scholarship, opening doors to education and new opportunities. Along the way, she battled depression, anxiety, and identity struggles, but each hardship only added to the depth of her testimony.

Her academic journey took her through four colleges, each chapter refining her purpose. Amid it all, she welcomed her son, DéVyon Collins, who became a powerful motivator in her pursuit of stability and success. After five years of unwavering commitment, Zanetta earned her B.A. in Psychology from Edward Waters College in Jacksonville, Florida. With her degree in hand but employment opportunities scarce, she took a bold step and enlisted in the U.S. Army.

Her military career ended early due to health problems, but it paved the way for a pivotal transformation. In 2009, Zanetta gave her life to Christ—a life-altering decision that became the cornerstone of her healing and self-discovery. Her journey of reinvention continued when she became a licensed cosmetologist, blending creativity with ministry. Over 16 years, Zanetta published six books through her publishing company, The Collins Christian Company, including Through My Eyes,

The Colors of My Wings, Once Broken, The Weight in the Wait, The Potter's Wheel, and In My Father's Hands.

Her book, *The Weight in the Wait,* caught the attention of Trilogy Publishing, a subsidiary of TBN, leading to its re-release on a larger platform. In addition to her writing, Zanetta helps other aspiring authors bring their stories to life, including the publication of *"Silence Her No More"* by Constance Burrell. After the devastating loss of her son in 2020, Zanetta came back with a vengeance to equip God's people with the tools needed to combat the tactics of the enemy, uproot and sever ties with the enemy! Her new literary work, "*InMy Father's Hands 2*", does just that! Her life is a living testimony of grace, grit, and God's unwavering faithfulness.

FOREWORD

God has entrusted Zanetta with sound, credible tools that will lead the captive to and through their freedom. In My Father's Hands 2: Breaking the Soul Ties of Sexual Sin is evidence of this truth. Zanetta's transparency invites and supports what the Father did for her; He is willing and able to do for others. It is a tool that provides hope and empowerment against bondage that once brought shame. There are practical, insightful, and proven steps to freedom.

Reading it, I was reminded of ***Revelations 2:11*** that we overcome by the blood of the lamb, the word of our testimony, and not living our lives unto death. A ready and repentant heart will embrace the victory they are believing for with unwavering faith in Christ's redemptive power.

Apostle, Dr. Shauna K. Jackson

IN MY FATHER'S HANDS 2

TABLE OF CONTENTS

DEDICATION iv
ABOUT v
FOREWORD viii
INTRODUCTION 1
CHAPTER ONE 4
Identifying The Orphan Spirit 4
CHAPTER TWO 12
The Spirit of Lust 12
CHAPTER THREE 16
Fornication 16
CHAPTER FOUR 23
Impurity 23
CHAPTER FIVE 27
Ungodly Soul Ties 27
CHAPTER SIX 39
Monitoring Spirits 39

CHAPTER SEVEN 44
Spiritual Warfare 44
CHAPTER EIGHT 50
Instruction 50
CHAPTER NINE 63
God's Armor 63
CHAPTER TEN 69
The Spirit of Adoption 69
CHAPTER ELEVEN 73
Prayer 73
Additional Prayers 78

INTRODUCTION

You know, when I first started writing books after coming to Christ, my first two books were a form of purging. Although the content was more explicit in nature, it was never my intent! As my life has evolved and seasons have changed, Christ has shaped and molded me; my books have become tools of impartation and deliverance. God has been having me continuously sift through the last 49 years of life, seemingly to leave no stone unturned. I see myself walking in a field of grass, waving my hands through it, looking for hidden things, such as sin, strongholds, soul ties, spiritual oppressors, and iniquities.

Any little thing that could stifle or hinder my walk with Him, so that I can ultimately be the best version of myself and He can continue using me for the uplifting of His Kingdom!

With that being said, the last book I wrote, *"In My Father's Hands, Where God Wants Us,"* was a book that was written out of immense grief and brokenness, after the untimely death of my son. The book became a roadmap not just for my continuous deliverance process, but for many others as well.

Now, I continue my journey with the hope of walking out my continued deliverance. It is also a tool that my Lord and Savior can use to draw other people out as well.

In this, now God has begun highlighting sexual sins to me! Yes, as I mentioned earlier, I have discussed them in my previous written works, but this time it's different! He is pushing me to study this topic more carefully: What are sexual sins? How do they show up in our lives? How have we all been involved in them? How can we recognize them? And how can we get rid of them?

So now let us continue mapping out our deliverance together because the word of God says:

For where two or three gather together as my followers, I am there among them."

Matthew 18:20

So, we can both be assured that our hearts are *"In Our Father's Hands!"*

Chapter One
IDENTIFYING THE ORPHAN SPIRIT

Here, I would probably have started initially with the Spirit of rejection. Since I discussed it extensively in my last book, I will only provide a brief summary of that Spirit.

"The core of the *spirit of rejection* is a deep-seated belief that one is not good enough or deserving of love and acceptance."

This develops due to destructive and demonic influences that lead to shame, lack of joy, and depression.

There are several ways to open the door to rejection. I'm only going to focus on one, and that is pre-marital sex/pregnancy. Think about it, if you are having sex outside of marriage. You are engaging in something God intended for a husband and wife. Marriage is a covenant or binding agreement between two parties. This is part of the reason God tells us not to have sex outside of marriage. Marriage is a covenant to God and is seen as being in "right" standing with Christ. On the other hand, engaging in sexual relations or intercourse/pregnancy outside of the covenant of marriage is considered impure in God's eyes, even though society sees it as the norm.

It is God's will that you should be sanctified: that you should avoid sexual immorality; that each of you should learn to control your own body in a way that is holy and honorable, not in passionate lust like the pagans, who do not know God; and that in this matter no one should wrong or take advantage of a brother or sister. The Lord will punish all those who commit such sins, as we told you and warned you before. For God did not call us to be impure, but to live a holy life.

Therefore, anyone who rejects this instruction does not reject a human being but God, the very God who gives you his Holy Spirit.

-1 Thessalonians 4:3-9

The consequences of engaging in pre-marital sex are extensive, and when it results in a child conceived outside of marriage, these repercussions extend far beyond, affecting generations to come. You may say or even think, 'What's the big deal?' The choice now leads to a defenseless child being born OUTSIDE the protection of the covenant, outside of a "covering!" To explain, I'll use something straightforward like car insurance; When you have car insurance, your vehicle isn't the only thing that's "covered," your physical person is also "covered." Meaning not only can your car get fixed because you have "coverage," but also your medical bills can be "covered". They can supply you with a rental car so that you are not stranded. But, without that insurance, your claim for everything that is supposed to be "covered" will be rejected because you are not in right standing with the insurance company. It's the same thing with Christ. So, having a baby outside the covenant of marriage means you are "uncovered" spiritually, which opens the door to the *Spirit of rejection.*

So now the foundation is set right? First, the *Spirit of rejection* creeps in; Then the "orphan spirit" enters. Even though the Bible doesn't use the term "*orphan spirit,*" it does discuss extensively *orphans:*

But you, God, see the trouble of the afflicted; you consider their grief and take it in hand. The victims commit themselves to you; you are the helper of the fatherless.

-Psalm 10:9

The *fatherless child*:

He defends the cause of the fatherless and the widow, and loves the foreigner residing among you, giving them food and clothing.

- Deuteronomy 10:18

And about the *Spirit of adoption!*

"I will not leave you as orphans; I will come to you".

- John 14:18

The *"orphan spirit"* attaches itself to someone who has experienced rejection throughout their life. In that *rejection*, they develop a *"stronghold"* in their minds!

A *stronghold* can be a physically fortified place, but for this subject matter, a *"stronghold"* represents a spiritual barrier within the mind. The stronghold embeds a false belief system and argues against the word of God.

"For the weapons of our warfare are not carnal but mighty in God for pulling down strongholds, casting down arguments and every high thing that exalts itself against the knowledge of God, bringing every thought into captivity to the obedience of Christ."

2 Corinthians 10:4-5

The *orphan spirit* will limit your capacity to identify who you are and whose you are. It also keeps you from operating fully in your purpose and potential. A prime example would be the parable of the prodigal son. In **Luke 15:11-32**, the younger son asks for his inheritance early and ultimately ends up poor and destitute. He even ate the same food as the pigs, having to return home with nothing! How can you know if you are operating in an orphan spirit?

These are some signs of an orphan spirit:

- The need to stand out (showboating)
- Competition
- Isolation
- Insecurity
- Fear
- Feelings of mistrust
- Resentment
- Anger
- Unable to receive correction

This is just a few examples. The *orphan spirit* also creates a bridge for a person to operate in self-indulgent behaviors, seeking gratification.

For example, shopaholics, addiction, gluttony, lust *(which, if you didn't know, the previous two are considered two of the deadly sins)*, and sex, just to name a few. All because you have not put your heart into *"In Your Father's Hands!"*

IN MY FATHER'S HANDS 2

Chapter Two
THE SPIRIT OF LUST

The Biblical definition of *lust* is, ***"a self-centered, disorderly desire for a sinful thing or an otherwise good thing in a sinful way, representing rebellion against God's authority and holiness."***

I think that was a great definition; don't you? The Spirit of *lust* is increasing exponentially more and more, the closer we get to the end times!

But the worries of this life, the deceitfulness of wealth, and the desires for other things come in and choke the word, making it unfruitful.

-Mark 4:19-

There are three types of l*ust* in the Bible, as listed in *1st John 2:16:*

1. The lust of the flesh

2. The lust of the eyes,
3. The pride of life.

The *lust* of the flesh: It is an excessive physical appetite, craving for certain physical desires to obtain gratification. For me, it was the act of homosexuality! Sit, see, and ask yourself, what is it for you?

The *lust* of the eyes: This version of *lust* is about seeing something and desiring it, which leads to the desire to possess something that's not yours, coveting, and jealousy. A simple example would be seeing a red Corvette that someone else is driving and wanting to have it for yourself.

The pride of life: The pride of life is defined as the human desire to be one's own God, which develops into greed (another of the seven deadly sins), a desire for personal glory, and ignorance.

For this book, we are going to talk about the first one, the *lust of the flesh*. Remember, the *lust of the flesh* is an excessive physical appetite, craving for certain physical desires to obtain gratification! Here are some characteristics or signs to look for in reference to the *Spirit of lust:*

- If a person acts as if they can't get enough of you…*LUST*
- All the person talks about is sex…<u>LUST</u>
- A person doesn't respect your boundaries…*LUST*
- If a person moves too quickly, typically…*LUST*

Side note for the last one: Unless it's in the season and timing of God! These things take place all because you have not put your heart, "*In Your Father's Hands!*"

IN MY FATHER'S HANDS 2

Chapter Three
FORNICATION

When the *Spirit of lust* enters, it then opens the door to *fornication*, better known as "*sexual sin.*" Fornication stems from the Greek word πορνεία (*Porneia*), which refers to a broad range of illicit sexual activity. The word also translates to sexual immorality, which is any sexual act outside the confines of a marriage between a man and a woman! During this study, I found something else interesting: the Greek word itself, "*porneia.*" The first half of that word is used in our language for watching porn or inappropriate things. So, if you break that word up,

- "*Porne*" means harlot or prostitute
- "*eia*" means to urge someone to action
- "*ia*" means the condition of being unconscious or a condition

When I see this, I recognize someone acting on unconscious urges toward illicit sexual behavior. This helps me understand why I struggled so badly with pornography after my son's death.

Let me explain, I had never been into porn. But after my son's death, I had this intolerable, insatiable desire to watch porn, even though I wasn't masturbating. It was the strangest thing to me, but I gained a better understanding of the natural world through my therapist.

Now, through my deeper spiritual studies, this revelation makes so much more sense! So now we've cleared that up; let's look at a list of things that fall under fornication & sexual sin:

- Adultery
- Homosexuality
- Incest
- Rape
- Sexual Violence
- Prostitution

Also, let me be very clear that I believe that there are those people who just make a choice to operate in such sin out of dealing with the *Spirit of rebellion.*

Furthermore, I believe that some people engage in these activities because of past incidents of being violated.

I can use myself as an example of both. So, let's start with examples of the "*spirit of rebellion.*" After the death of my son, I couldn't wrap my head around the fact that he had gone!

I couldn't wrap my mind around the fact that here I am living my life right to the best of my knowledge and per the word of God, yet my son was taken senselessly from me.

Deuteronomy 30:19: Today I have given you the choice between life and death, between blessings and curses. Now I call on heaven and earth to witness the choice you make.

Oh, that you would choose life, so that you and your descendants might live!

How was this possible when I had been told that my son was going to be okay? I couldn't conceive that he was dead! As a result, I became angry and rebellious about the fact that my son was gone! Now, in these scenarios, there were also other spiritual factors at play, such as monitoring spirits, which we will discuss later. I felt like I couldn't trust God anymore! But that was because I was looking with my natural eyes, not my spiritual ones!

So, we fix our eyes not on what is seen, but on what is unseen, since what is seen is temporary, but what is unseen is eternal".

-2 Corinthians 4:18-

So, in that I said, "screw it, I am going to live my life," in short, I turned back to my old ways:

They prove the truth of this proverb: "A dog returns to its vomit." And another says, "A washed pig returns to the mud."

-2 Peter 2:22-

And just like that, after 14 years of abstaining from sex, I slept with someone very dear to me, which I discussed more in-depth in my last book. But nevertheless, that's the first example of me falling back into homosexuality, sexual sin, and fornication!

The second example is of me being molested as a little girl! You may ask, how does your getting molested make you fall into sexual sin? Don't worry, I'll elaborate! So, I was molested by one of my family members between the ages of four and five. Again, I've talked about it in one of my previous books, but in that book, a door was open to incest. Incest is a sexual act between relatives, which is on the list above! Again, it was not done by my hands, nor was it my fault! So, if you are reading this and you were molested, it's never your fault!

In hindsight, that one act of being violated not only shifted my desires for an increased sexual appetite, but it also warped my choices later on in life. I absolutely didn't trust men. At one point, I began dating someone younger than me. No, she wasn't a child, but she was younger than me! Now, I had permission from her family to date her. In my mind, because I had permission, it seemed appropriate. But was it okay? Was it acceptable according to the word of God?

You say, "I am allowed to do anything"— but not everything is good for you. And even though "I am allowed to do anything," I must not become a slave to anything.

- 1 Corinthians 6:12-

So, I pose the question again: Was it right? Nope, not by any means! Why, because I had not put my heart "*In my father's hands.*"

IN MY FATHER'S HANDS 2

Chapter Four
IMPURITY

Impurity represents a state of being morally or ceremonially unclean. In this book, we will explore the moral implications of being unclean. Furthermore, we will explore its connection to the spiritual realm, as well as its association with defilement, sin, and corruption. Finally, we will discuss how impurity affects us spiritually and separates us from God's Holiness!

He went on: "What comes out of a person is what defiles them. For it is from within, out of a person's heart, that evil thoughts come

—sexual immorality, theft, murder, adultery, greed, malice, deceit, lewdness, envy, slander, arrogance, and folly. All these evils come from inside and defile a person."

-Mark 7:20-23

Impurity prevents a person from having a close relationship with God because it creates a barrier between you and Christ. That barrier not only hinders your spiritual growth. But it can also: separate you from Christ, separate you from God's presence, weaken your spiritual powers, and steal your spiritual joy!

When operating in *impurity,* you can not only defile your physical body but also forfeit your spiritual inheritance. In retrospect, I realized that it can also damage (blemish) your testimony, which is exactly what I did when I went back to the vomit, after the death of my son!

They prove the truth of this proverb: "A dog returns to its vomit." And another says, "A washed pig returns to the mud."

- 2 Peter: 2:22

And I had additional old things to return, as well as new things. Remember that when you make changes in your life and remove evil entities, spirits, or influences from your life, you then turn around and allow those same spirits to return. They return stronger, accompanied by additional spirits, which attempt to take over and dwell within you.

"When an evilspirit leaves a person, it goes into the desert, searching for rest. But when it finds none, it says, 'I will return to the person I came from.' So, it returns and finds that its former home is all swept and in order. Then the Spirit finds seven other spirits more evil than itself, and they all enter the person and live there. And so that person is worse off than before."

Luke 11:24-26

All because I had not put my heart, "*In My Father's Hands.*"

IN MY FATHER'S HANDS 2

CHAPTER FIVE
UNGODLY SOUL TIES

My definition of *"soul ties"* is exactly what it looks like: two souls tied together (like an umbilical cord still attached to the mother after giving birth). Biblically, similar to *"the orphan spirit,"* the term *"soul ties"* is not explicitly used in the Bible. However, the term describes having a deep emotional connection between two individuals, which can be in a healthy context, as in **Genesis 2:24**

This explains why a man leaves his Father and mother and is joined to his wife, and the two are united into one.

On the other hand, soul ties can have an unhealthy context, as in **1 Samuel 18:1-30**, which talks about Jonathan being knit with David's soul:

After David had finished talking with Saul, he met Jonathan, the King's son. There was an immediate bond between them, for Jonathan loved David. From that day on, Saul kept David with him and wouldn't let him return home. And Jonathan made a solemn pact with David, because he loved him as he loved himself. Jonathan sealed the pact by taking off his robe and giving it to David, together with his tunic, sword, bow, and belt.

Whatever Saul asked David to do, David did it successfully. So Saul made him a commander over the men of war, an appointment that was welcomed by both the people and Saul's officers.

When the victorious Israelite army was returning home after David had killed the Philistine, women from all the towns of Israel came out to meet King Saul. They sang and danced with joy, accompanied by tambourines and cymbals.

This was their song: "Saul has killed his thousands, and David his ten thousands!"

This made Saul very angry. "What's this?" he said. "They credit David with ten thousand and me with only thousands.

Next, they'll be making him their King! From that time on, Saul kept a jealous eye on David.

The very next day, a tormenting spirit from God overwhelmed Saul, and he began to rave in his house like a madman. David was playing the harp, as he did each day. But Saul had a spear in his hand, and he suddenly hurled it at David, intending to pin him to the wall. But David escaped him twice.

Saul was then afraid of David, for the Lord was with David and had turned away from Saul. Finally, Saul sent him away and appointed him commander over 1,000 men, and David faithfully led his troops into battle.

David continued to succeed in everything he did, for the Lord was with him. When Saul recognized this, he became even more afraid of him. But all Israel and Judah loved David because he was so successful at leading his troops into battle.

One day, Saul said to David, "I am ready to give you my older daughter, Merab, as your wife. But first you must prove yourself to be a real warrior by fighting the Lord's battles." For Saul thought, "I'll send him out against the Philistines and let them kill him rather than doing it myself."

"Who am I, and what is my family in Israel that I should be the king's son-in-law?" David exclaimed. "My father's family is nothing!"

So when the time came for Saul to give his daughter Merab in marriage to David, he gave her instead to Adriel, a man from Meholah.

In the meantime, Saul's daughter Michal had fallen in love with David, and Saul was delighted when he heard about it. "Here's another chance to see him killed by the Philistines!" Saul said to himself. But to David he said, "Today you have a second chance to become my son-in-law!"

Then Saul told his men to say to David, "The King really likes you, and so do we. Why don't you accept the King's offer and become his son-in-law?"

When Saul's men said these things to David, he replied, "How can a poor man from a humble family afford the bride price for the daughter of a king?"

When Saul's men reported this back to the King, he told them, "Tell David that all I want for the bride price is 100 Philistine foreskins! Vengeance on my enemies is all I really want." But what Saul had in mind was that David would be killed in the fight.

David was delighted to accept the offer. Before the time limit expired, he and his men went out and killed 200 Philistines. Then David fulfilled the King's requirement by presenting all their foreskins to him. So Saul gave his daughter Michal to David to be his wife.

When Saul realized that the Lord was with David and how much his daughter Michal loved him, Saul became even more afraid of him. He remained David's enemy for the rest of his life.

Every time the commanders of the Philistines attacked, David was more successful against them than all the rest of Saul's officers. So David's name became very famous.

Since we are discussing the breaking of *soul ties* of *sexual sin*, of course, we are going to discuss the unhealthy version.

Now, when we started this book, I told you that God had had me sifting through the weeds to ensure that I left no stone unturned. He's been mapping this thing out for me.

First, the *Spirit of rejection*, which led to the *orphan spirit,* from the *orphan spirit,* which happens when a person is motherless and/or fatherless.

Realistically, someone can just *feel* abandoned, and that spirit will take residence like a squatter in an abandoned home. This was definitely the case with me. This became the doorway for the enemy to entangle me and reinject the *Spirit of lust*.

In my studies, I discovered that I operated in the *lust of the eyes* as well. *Why* do I feel this way? My revelation about the *lust of the eyes* took me back to my relationship with my parents, or should I say the lack thereof! I remember often seeing other people's families that seemed to be the "*perfect family*." I desired that for myself. I would romanticize about having a family of my own first, and my husband would be my knight in shining armor! Instead, because of the childhood sexual violation, it fostered my distrust of men and flamed the fire that burned up my innocence. Those ashes birthed a doorway to the *Spirit of homosexuality*. Instead of the clichéd picket fence and a nuclear family, I boldly replaced that childhood fantasy of a wife as my spouse. Thankfully, God said, "No, you are not!" I now understand that faulty thinking patterns built a stronghold in my mind regarding how I view family and relationships. I felt like, since I didn't have one of my own, I was going to recreate my own warped and distorted version. It felt so right to me at that time!

Let me continue. He then explained fornication to me, and while the molestation wasn't my fault, it opened a door to an unnatural, unholy sexual desire that caused me to align myself with darkness. From *fornication* still guiding me along this map, sifting through weeds. He leads me to impurity again, which basically means being unclean spiritually! All the hardships I've faced—some of which I brought upon myself—planted spiritual forces within me that were either never meant for me or came at the wrong time, outside of God's covenant and purpose.

As I stated, when my son was killed, I said, "Screw it, I am going to live my life!" I turned back to my old life likelot's wife to indulging in homosexuality! Although it was only for a short period of time because God rebuked me in love, saying, "No, my daughter, this isn't you anymore!" But in that short period of time, I developed an *ungodly soul tie*. I employ you to read more of *1 Samuel 18,* starting at *verse 8*. It explains how Saul became very angry with David because of a song that was created in celebration of David's conquests. This tormented Saul…i.e., *soul ties* lead to an unhealthy, ungodly attachment!

This made Saul very angry. "What's this?" he said.

"They credit David with ten thousand and me with only thousands. Next, they'll be making him their King!" From that time on, Saul kept a jealous eye on David.

The very next day, a tormenting spirit from God overwhelmed Saul, and he began to rave in his house like a madman. David was playing the harp, as he did each day. But Saul had a spear in his hand, and he suddenly hurled it at David, intending to pin him to the wall. But David escaped him twice.

Saul was then afraid of David, for the Lord was with David and had turned away from Saul. Finally, Saul sent him away and appointed him commander over 1,000 men, and David faithfully led his troops into battle.

-1 Samuel 18:8-13-

I developed an *ungodly soul tie* operating in *sexual immorality & sin*. Something I had walked away from earlier in my walk with Christ, because of my disobedience and rebellion towards God! I, me, Zanetta, walked back into that door. This decision perverted my emotions, my decision-making, and my spiritual life. Not surprisingly, it also began making me physically sick because sometimes a sick soul leads to a sick body! The spiritual does impact the natural, and what happened to me is an indication of this.

It got to a point where internally I felt as if I was dying inside. It is because the oppression was taking a toll on me spiritually! I was embarrassed to say the least! All because I had not put my heart, *"In My Father's Hands!"*

IN MY FATHER'S HANDS 2

Chapter Six
MONITORING SPIRITS

After God took me through *Ungodly Soul Ties*, He then shifted my focus to *monitoring spirits!* A *monitoring spirit* is described Biblically as demonic forces that observe, a demonic intelligence network that oppresses believers. Remember, I said, I felt oppressed?

Then the Lord asked Satan, "Have you noticed my servant Job? He is the finest man in all the earth. He is blameless—a man of complete integrity. He fears God and stays away from evil."

Satan replied to the Lord, "Yes, but Job has good reason to fear God. You have always put a wall of protection around him and his home and his property. You have made him prosper in everything he does. Look how rich he is! But reach out and take away everything he has, and he will surely curse you to your face!"

"All right, you may test him," the Lord said to Satan. "Do whatever you want with everything he possesses, but don't harm him physically." So, Satan left the Lord's presence.

-Job 1:8-15-

Monitoring spirits are considered to be supernatural entities that surveil and "watch" you spiritually, reporting on your life to the enemy. This act is intended to hinder or disrupt your spiritual walk. They are not just passively sitting by watching, either; they are very strategic. To explain, they operate using your traits, routines, prayers, and even your emotions to create destructive loopholes to tear you down! I am sure you're asking, Zanetta, how are we being monitored?

I am glad you asked! You can be monitored in several different ways:

- Familiar Spirits

- Spying dreams
- Astro projection/ Out of body Experiences
- Objects
- People
- Evil animals and birds, like goats, snakes, cats, lizards, frogs, and owls, just to name a few.

Monitoring spirits can torment you through any or all of the following:

- Recurring nightmare
- Unexplained setbacks, personally or professionally
- Feeling uneasy or anxious

I realize now that I had definitely been under surveillance, being strategically watched by a monitoring spirit.

Do not revile the King even in your thoughts, or curse the rich in your bedroom, because a bird in the sky may carry your words, and a bird on the wing may report what you say.

- Ecclesiastes 10:20

All because I had not put my heart, "In My Father's Hands." What about you? Do you think you have been monitored?

IN MY FATHER'S HANDS 2

Chapter Seven
SPIRITUAL WARFARE

Before we discuss spiritual warfare, we must first discuss the roles of angels, demons, principalities, household wickedness, marine spirits, occult powers, and their relationships. Biblically speaking, demons seek you out to destroy you,

For weare not fighting against flesh-and-blood enemies, but against evil rulers and authorities of the unseen world, against mighty powers in this dark world, and against evil spirits in the heavenly places

-Ephesians 6:12

However, the reverse side of that is that angels are sent to protect you, and they are messengers of Christ.

You alone are the Lord. You made the skies and the heavens and all the stars. You made the earth and the seas and everything in them. You preserve them all, and the angels of heaven worship you.

-Nehemiah 9:6

Principalities are considered to be high-ranking, demonic forces that work for the enemy to oppose God's purposes.

Household wickedness refers to various behaviors and destructive influences that originate within one's own family—for example, behaviors such as jealousy, envy, and betrayal. A prime example is Cain and Abel in Chapter 4 of *Genesis*.

Marine Spirits are demonic entities that function from bodies of water and can affect or hinder a person's life spiritually through sexual perversions, spiritual spouses, incubi, and succubi.

On that day, the LORD will take his terrible, swift sword and punish Leviathan, the swiftly

moving serpent, the coiling, writhing serpent. He will kill the dragon of the sea.....

Isaiah 27:1

Magic is considered to be the power of being able to influence a course of events by the use of supernatural forces. Power is used by a person to control events or other people.

It's also related to witchcraft, necromancy, enchantment, spiritualism, and sorcery, to name a few. These practices date back to the Garden of Eden, when the enemy disguised himself as a talking snake in the third chapter of Genesis. Now that we have a deeper understanding of some of the tools the enemy uses during spiritual warfare, we can proceed.

Now we can delve more deeply into it; in the Bible, *spiritual warfare* is considered a battle against evil spiritual forces. Spiritual warfare takes place in the spiritual realm on a legal battlefield, designed to be an intentional and calculated spiritual place opened through legal loopholes, windows, ignorance, and carelessness, used to hijack glory, dreams, and siphon favor. Ultimately, spiritual warfare targets a person's destiny!

Signs of spiritual warfare include, but are not limited to:

- Loss of spiritual desire
- Pulling away from God
- Returning to old habits
- Great sensitivity to spiritual atmosphere
- Unusual Aversity
- Intense Temptation

Now, this is just to name a few; there are several more. Additionally, please note that not everything falls under the category of *spiritual warfare*.

It is also important to understand why spiritual warfare occurs. You may ask why? Some reasons include:

1. **Cultural influences:** You often hear in the African American Community about people making statements about their ancestors or their roots, not knowing that some of our ancestors operated witchcraft, which led to generational curses. And now you may be left to deal with the sins of your ancestors through spiritual warfare.
2. **Internal struggles or personal sin:** This is the internal battle within, ethical dilemmas that can often lead to spiritual battles internally.
3. **Spiritual Growth:** The more someone searches for a deeper understanding spiritually, the more challenges that arise attempting to stunt their growth spiritually, if you will!

This happens because the enemy is trying to keep you from completely putting your heart, "*In Your Father's Hands!*

IN MY FATHER'S HANDS 2

Chapter Eight
INSTRUCTION

Let me say that if you've gotten this far, you should've noticed that I have no problem using my life as a tool that can be used as a backdrop to orchestrate someone's freedom. Why? Because I believe it's what God has called me to do.

Secondly, if you've made it this far, I'd venture to say that you desire change; perhaps you've reached the end of yourself. You are searching for tools that can help you move into alignment with what God has in store for your life, for your purpose.

So, with that being said, we've continued sifting through this grass looking for stones that may have been overlooked or just never found until the most opportune time *(God's Timing),* and we are here! He has identified some things, and He has also given us some tools.

So, now let us blueprint our strategy! The first thing we are going to identify and acknowledge.

1. Identify & Acknowledge

What are we identifying and acknowledging, you may ask? Whatever *sexual sin* has created a *soul tie* through an ungodly connection. You have to be able to identify the patterns, emotional connections, and/or persons that have been hindering your walk with Christ. Again, I'll use my past as an example. For me, one of the biggest issues in my walk with Christ has been dealing with the Spirit *of homosexuality*. I would spend extensive periods of time with no feelings whatsoever in reference to the subject matter. Then boom, it would hit me like a ton of bricks, and I was always so confused about that.

In my heart of hearts, I knew I was delivered from that Spirit.So, why did it keep resurfacing in my life? Well, first of all, the enemy's Job is to utilize tactics to keep us off our path to purpose:

Then Peter called to him, "Lord, if it's really you, tell me to come to you, walking on the water."

"Yes, come," Jesus said.

So, Peter went over the side of the boat and walked on the water toward Jesus. But when he saw the strong wind and the waves, he was terrified and began to sink. "Save me, Lord!" he shouted.

Jesus immediately reached out and grabbed him. "You have so little faith," Jesus said. "Why did you doubt me?"

-Matthew 14:28-31

Secondly, God commands us to operate in *self-control*, which is also one of the fruits of the Spirit, as mentioned in Galatians 5:22-23.

So, prepare your minds for action and exercise self-control. Put all your hope in the gracious salvation that will come to you when Jesus Christ is revealed to the world.

-1 Peter 1:13

Before we move on, let me be very clear that my walk hasn't been riddled with making the same mistake over and over again! However, as I said, there were still some stones that needed to be turned over, so that I could say, "This devil I will see no more!"

Then the devil, who had deceived them, was thrown into the fiery lake of burning sulfur, joining the beast and the false prophet.

There they will be tormented day and night forever and ever.

-Revelations 20:10

So, again, number one was identify, and I've done that. Now you do the same!

Something else I did was identify not just every woman I had ever slept with, but every man as well. You must remember that if the intercourse is outside of the confines of marriage, it's also considered a sin, and you risk the chance of creating a *soul tie*!

Now, you need to do the same thing: get a piece of paper or use the space below this chapter, sit, see, and identify!

2. Confess

The word *confess* (Greek: *xenologer*, Strong's G1843) means "to declare, say out loud, exclaim, divulge, or profess." So, confess what your sexual sin is! Because when you confess, the enemy loses his power. He has nothing to hold over your head because it's out in the open. Now, yes, you can confess out loud to yourself. However, in my opinion, it's also advisable to confess to your leadership, so they know how to pray for you. The Bible says,

Whoever conceals their sins does not prosper, but the one who confesses and renounces them finds mercy.

—Proverbs 28:13

Additionally, confessing holds you to a higher level of accountability. If you have the right leadership, they will hold you to the fire, respectfully, of course.

Brothers and sisters, if someone is caught in a sin, you who live by the Spirit should restore that person gently. But watch yourselves, or you also may be tempted. Carry each other's burdens, and in this way you will fulfill the law of Christ.

-Galatians 6:1-2

3. Renounce the Tie

The definition of renounce means to disclaim or reject something formally!

For example, sin, worldly desires, or something that you came into agreement with, knowingly or unknowingly, just to name a few. Therefore, ensure that you verbally declare that you no longer agree with the ungodly connection and reject its influence over your life.

The grace of God that brings salvation has appeared to all people, teaching us to deny

ungodliness and worldly desires, and to live a self-controlled, upright, and godly life in the present age

-Titus 2:11-12

4. Forgive

Now this one is a two-part action because it's not just for you, but the other party as well. You have to let go of anger, pray for God's healing, release negative effects, and you have to forgive yourself for the part that you played in the situation!

If you forgive those who sin against you, your heavenly Father will forgive you.

-Matthew 6:14

And

If we confess our sins, he is faithful and just to forgive us our sins and to cleanse us from all unrighteousness

-1 John 1:9

5. Sever the ties

Ask Jesus for His blood to break the connection and sever the link between your soul and theirs, out loud! Another key component is written in ***Ecclesiastes 12:6-8**.* You must sever the silver cord between you and the sexual sin!

Yes, remember your Creator now while you are young, before the silver cord of life snaps and the golden bowl is broken. Don't wait until the water jar is smashed at the spring and the pulley is broken at the well. For then the dust will return to the earth, and the Spirit will return to God who gave it."Everything is meaningless," says the Teacher, "completely meaningless."

Again, for me, it was homosexuality. What is it for you? What is the silver cord, you may ask? The silver cord is used as a metaphor for death. It is thought to be a connection, a cord that nourishes our spirits as well as sustains our physical bodies. It keeps our spirits within it, just like an umbilical cord.

Severing the silver cord restores us to Christ or to whatever God you serve. Interestingly, the silver cord appears only once in the Bible. How do you sever this cord? If you have ungodly, illicit, and illegal soul ties—past or present—each one must be loosed, snapped, broken, burned, severed, and shattered to achieve divine breakthrough and freedom. How do you do this, you might ask?

At this point, you then pick up the sword of the Spirit, which is the word of God.

The sword of the Spirit is the number one offensive tool in your arsenal when combating spiritual warfare! It is used to defend and combat the enemy! For me, as I pray the word of God, it's as if I am wielding a natural sword, even though this is done spiritually. While praying the word of God, I walk as if I am literally slicing something to shreds while declaring God's word, as if I were in a fencing contest!

After that, you proceed to the next step.

6. Burn the spiritual altars

This is done to destroy symbolically through prayer that calls forth the "fire of God" to destroy demonic altars, breaking demonic covenants that you have come into agreement with, breaking spiritual attacks, and spiritual strongholds!

7. Seal the door

Close and seal the spiritual door that was once opened by the *soul tie* and the sin. Renounce any demonic access points that were created in the relationship to prevent any harmful influences.

After that, decree that you are cutting the soul ties, and ask for the door to be sealed by the blood of Jesus!

But the blood on your doorposts will serve as a sign, marking the houses where you are staying. When I see the blood, I will pass over you. This plague of death will not touch you when I strike the land of Egypt.

-Exodus 12:13

8. Remove all physical connections

Get rid of everything that remains of the relationships, pictures, souvenirs, and gifts.

You must burn their idols in fire, and you must not covet the silver or gold that covers them.

You must not take it, or it will become a trap to you, for it is detestable to the Lord your God. Do not bring any detestable objects into your home, for then you will be destroyed, just like them. You must utterly detest such things, for they are set apart for destruction.

-Deuteronomy 7:25-26

9. Heal & rebuild

Set healthy boundaries, seek support, renew your mindset, and pursue Godly connections so that you can put your heart back "*In Your Father's Hands!*"

He heals the brokenhearted and bandages their wounds.

-Psalm 147:

IN MY FATHER'S HANDS 2

CHAPTER NINE
GOD'S ARMOR

After following all those steps, it's now time to put on the whole *Armor of God!*

What is the "*Whole Armor of God?*" In Ephesians, Apostle Paul was incarcerated, but he was still addressing the church in Ephesus, giving them instructions on their spiritual and social duties. For example, he discussed the responsibilities in work, family, and prayer.In that, he described a metaphor about the"*Armor of God!*" The discussion referenced spiritual tools that Christians should use to defend themselves spiritually against the enemy.

A final word: Be strong in the Lord and in his mighty power.[11] Put on all of God's armor so that you will be able to stand firm against all strategies of the devil. For we are not fighting against flesh-and-blood enemies, but against evil rulers and authorities of the unseen world, against mighty powers in this dark world, and against evil spirits in the heavenly places.

Therefore, put on every piece of God's armor so you will be able to resist the enemy in the time of evil. Then, after the battle, you will still be standing firm. Stand your ground, putting on the belt of truth and the body armor of God's righteousness. [15] For shoes, put on the peace that comes from the Good News so that you will be fully prepared. In addition to all of these, hold up the shield of faith to stop the fiery arrows of the devil. Put on salvation as your helmet, and take the sword of the Spirit, which is the word of God.

Pray in the Spirit at all times and on every occasion. Stay alert and be persistent in your prayers for all believers everywhere.

-Ephesians 6:10-18

All of these are important when dealing with deliverance and spiritual warfare!

The Sword of the Spirit: The *Sword of the Spirit* is used against lies.

For example, in my case, the enemy has tried to convince me for years that I wasn't free from homosexuality, but the word of God/ *Sword of the Spirit* says that I am!

For sin shall not have dominion over you, for you are not under the law, but under grace

-Romans 6:14

Spiritual Decrement: It's used to measure the spiritual toll that helps a believer make sound decisions.

And this is my prayer: that your love may abound more and more in knowledge and depth of insight, [10] so that you may be able to discern what is best and may be pure and blameless for the day of Christ,

- Philippians 1:9-10

Now, some say there are "*seven spirits of discernment,*" but I am not 100 percent sure about that statement. Some people say that's a misinterpretation of the phrase, "*The Seven Spirits of God,*" God's attributes, which include:

- Wisdom
- Knowledge
- Counsel
- Understanding
- Strength
- Fear of God

I can see where or how the confusion has been amplified, but I can also see how each of the tools listed above could fall under spiritual decrement.

It is also used for Ministerial Preparation.

2 Timothy 3:16-17states the sword helps train us, correct us, rebuke us, and equip us for ministry!

Defense against temptation

The *Sword of the Spirit* is also adefense against temptation. The *Sword of the Spirit*, again, which is the word of God, combats temptations with the use of the scripture.

So, we have this vital information; we must remember to utilize it. When we pray, we should remember all of them, but most importantly, not forget to armor ourselves with the sword of the S*pirit*! In doing so, we can be certain that our hearts are, "*In Our Father's Hands!*"

IN MY FATHER'S HANDS 2

Chapter Ten
THE SPIRIT OF ADOPTION

We are going to circle back! More than likely, as a believer or not, nine out of ten times, you may have dealt with the *Spirit of rejection* as well as the *orphan spirit*. Both spirits opened you up to a lot of what we have discussed in this book. However, now you have the instructions, the roadmap, and the tools necessary to dismantle the enemy's plan!

Let's delve into the *Spirit of adoption*! What is the *Spirit of adoption?* The *Spirit of adoption* is one in which you surrender your life to Christ and are adopted into Christ.

As a Gentile, if you are not of Jewish ethnicity, the spiritual adoption process confirms your sonship in Christ. In other words, you are an official child of God with all the rights afforded to you! This enables you as a believer to have an intimate relationship with the Father, Son, and the Holy Spirit! The *Spirit of adoption* also:

- Provides Confidence
- Offer assurance in your suffering
- Replaces Fear with Love

As a result, now you have someone that you can call on, someone who has "a*dopted*" you, even though you have been rejected or may have been an orphan! You now have the right to call on, "*Abba, Father,*"all because you followed the road map and secured your heart, *"In Your Father's Hands!"*

Therefore, dear brothers and sisters, you have no obligation to do what your sinful nature urges you to do. For if you live by its dictates, you will die. But if through the power of the Spirit you put to death the deeds of your sinful nature, you will live. For all whom the Spirit of God leads are childrenof God.

So you have not received a spirit that makes you fearful slaves. Instead, you received God's Spirit when he adopted you as his own children.

Now we call him, "Abba, Father." For his Spirit joins with our Spirit to affirm that we are God's children. And since we are his children, we are his heirs. In fact, together with Christ, we are heirs of God's glory. But if we are to share his glory, we must also share his suffering.

-Romans 8:12-17

IN MY FATHER'S HANDS 2

Chapter Eleven
PRAYER

Now, it's time to go into your war room and abolish all forms of sexual sin! I don't care if you consider yourself gay, bisexual, straight, or anything in between; prayer will be the gateway to true freedom. The stage is now set for each one of us to start cutting every soul tie with every individual we have ever slept with, even if you don't remember their names! I wrote this prayer out so that I would have a physical copy to ensure that I wouldn't leave any stone unturned after sifting through all the challenges that God had me walking through on this roadmap to deliverance. The prayer is written in the first person, but modify or change it as needed to fit your needs. Let's pray!

I come before you humbly, as I know how asking for forgiveness for things that I know I've done wrong, because, against you, and you alone, have I sinned. I have done what is evil in your sight. For I recognize my rebellion, and it haunts me day and night.

You will be proved right in what you say, and your judgment against. I also come before you for things unknown or that I can't remember. I thank you, Father, for having an open ear to hear and receive my prayers as my heart's cries for repentance, for complete and total deliverance!

I pray that you have mercy on me because of your unfailing love! I acknowledge the fact that I have operated in homosexual acts/fornication (whatever your sexual sin was or is), which have created ungodly soul ties in my life!

I realize that *fornication* and any homosexual act is a detestable sin *(remember to add in your sexual sin here, all sexual acts outside the bounds of marriage).*

I am thankful that I can confess my sins as well as identify the negative patterns and emotional hold that each of these relationships has ever had on me. (Here is where you call out the names of each individual that you slept with, but also ask God to cover them all in prayer, even those you can't remember!)

I stand before you, Father God, renouncing/denouncing any and every agreement that I have aligned with during each and every ungodly connection, and I reject the influence that it has had over my life! Father God, I hold no resentment or anger in my heart towards anyone, including myself! I pray right now for healing and a release of any effects from my past relationships.

I hold in my spiritual hands the sword of the Spirit (your word), as written in Ephesians 6:17, and I see the silver cord, as discussed in Ecclesiastes 12:6-8, that I have attached myself to spiritually, and it has yielded ungodly soul ties/connections that need to be severed. So, I stand before the sovereign King and take up my sword and I decree and declare that the blood of Jesus goes before me and the sliver cord and every single ungodly soul tie in my lives is now, loosed, broken, sliced and severed, and shattered between me and each person on my list known and unknown, in the matchless name of Jesus Christ!

I close every single door and demonic access points that were opened by my choices, and I seal them with the blood of Jesus Christ!

I uproot, bind, and cast out both the Spirit of rejection and the orphan spirit! I decree and declare that through the Spirit of adoption.

I have confirmed my sonship in Christ. I am born again, I am not a corruptible seed, I control my own body and my mind.

Sin does not reign in my body, and anything that is not of God is subject to death, and I kill it right now! I am incorruptible and holy by the word of God! And the power of sin is broken off of my life, and I live in honor and holiness!

I put on the Belt of Truth to operate in continuous integrity. The Breastplate of Righteousness, to protect my heart against any form of sin. The Shield of Faith, to protect me from temptation and doubts!

I pray God that because of your unfailing love and compassion, you'll blot out the stain of my sins. Wash me clean from my guilt. Purify me from my sin.

I put on the Shoes of the Gospel of Peace, signifying my readiness to spread the message of preparation and peace, and to stand firmly in my faith in the matchless name of Jesus. I pray, Amen!

There is also a book by Timothy Atunnise entitled, "Spiritual Criminals Identified and Arrested. This book serves as a blueprint for freedom. It's an amazing tool that you can utilize for real freedom, if you so desire, for yourself and others. Additionally, I am going to create a list of additional prayers from that book that I feel deal with "Breaking the Soul Ties of Sexual Sin!" I recommend that anyone walking out of their deliverance, not just in sexual sin, but in every area of their life, purchase this book!

Additional Prayers

1. "In the name of Jesus, I decree every thief of my destiny, virtue, and finances be exposed and arrested. I recovered all that was stolen from me seven years ago. Fold restoration, supernatural acceleration, and divine compensation shall be my portion now. Atunnise, T. (2025). *Spiritual Criminals Identified & Arrested*. Independently Published.
2. I'll take authority over every spiritual robber attacking my career, relationships, or health. Let their operations scatter. I possess my inheritance, reclaim my space, and silence

every voice declaring lack and limitations over my life in Jesus' mighty name. Atunnise, T. (2025). *Spiritual Criminals Identified & Arrested*. Independently Published.

3. I command every spiritual death aside to my lineage to be arrested. Let the divine hands of God restore my family's virtue and bestow generational blessings upon us. The blood of Jesus now breaks the cycle of theft and dryness. Atunnise, T. (2025). *Spiritual Criminals Identified & Arrested*. Independently Published.

4. In the name of Jesus, I recover my wasted years, stolen dreams, and hijack potential. Every demonic exchange made against me is reversed. I rise in strength, clarity, and purpose to fulfill my divine assignment without delay. Atunnise, T. (2025). *Spiritual Criminals Identified & Arrested*. Independently Published.

5. I speak to every lost opportunity buried by witchcraft manipulation resurrected now. Let the voice of the blood of Jesus speak

restoration. My days of struggling are over. I walk boldly into God's prepared blessings, untouched and unaltered. Atunnise, T. (2025). *Spiritual Criminals Identified & Arrested.* Independently Published.

6. I command powers that specialize in spiritual theft through dreams, encounters, or transactions to be silenced forever. Let the fire of God expose your networks. I decree I will sleep in safety, rise in strength, and my portion shall no longer be touched. Atunnise, T. (2025). *Spiritual Criminals Identified & Arrested.* Independently Published.

7. I command every delay orchestrated by stolen virtues, and disconnections break now. Divine Speedy enters my life. The wasted time is reversed. I declare that this is my time of manifestation and the manifestation of visual evidence of restoration in the name of Jesus. Atunnise, T. (2025). *Spiritual Criminals Identified & Arrested.* Independently Published.

8. I speak to every star that was down, every light that was covered, and every voice that was silent to arise. Shine again! Burn brighter! The enemy shall not hide or control my life anymore in Jesus' name. Atunnise, T. (2025). *Spiritual Criminals Identified & Arrested.* Independently Published.
9. I commend a divine recall of everything stolen from me in my childhood, youth, or ignorance. Let nothing be wasted. Every virtue, gift, and mental hijacked or buried return now to my life with power and increase in Jesus' name. Atunnise, T. (2025). *Spiritual Criminals Identified & Arrested.* Independently Published.
10. I decree all evil seeds planted during vulnerable moments through trauma, sleep, or manipulation, or overturn; I declare divine justice and replacement by seeds of healing, wisdom, and restoration that show you testimonies too great to be silenced. Atunnise,

T. (2025). *Spiritual Criminals Identified & Arrested*. Independently Published.

11. I command that every demonic transaction done on evil altars with my name, destiny, or bloodline be revoked. The blood of Jesus speaks louder. I cancel the thief's legal right. My name is cleared. My destiny is defended. My breakthrough is secure. Atunnise, T. (2025). *Spiritual Criminals Identified & Arrested*. Independently Published.

12. I decree divine insurance over my destiny. No more spiritual burglary. My purpose is sealed, my gates are fortified, and every blessing with my name on it finds me, untouched and overflowing, now and forever in the name of Jesus. Atunnise, T. (2025). *Spiritual Criminals Identified & Arrested*. Independently Published.

13. In the name of Jesus, I take back my true identity from every spiritual thief and hijacker. I declare I am who God says I am, walking in divine purpose, destiny, and calling without confusion or delay. Atunnise, T.

(2025). *Spiritual Criminals Identified & Arrested.* Independently Published.

14. Every identity-swapping altar speaking against my destiny is now silenced by the blood of Jesus. I reject every false label placed on me and declare restoration of my divine name, row, and assignment from heaven. Atunnise, T. (2025). *Spiritual Criminals Identified & Arrested.* Independently Published.

15. I command every evil hand that rewrote my spiritual identity to be cut off by fire. I reclaim my original spiritual blueprint and declare the full restoration of divine recognition and purpose in my life. Atunnise, T. (2025). *Spiritual Criminals Identified & Arrested.* Independently Published.

16. By the power in the name of Jesus, I cancel every demonic exchange made in my dreams or ignorance. I retrieve my stolen virtual and clear that heaven's original script for my life shall manifest in full. Atunnise, T.

(2025). *Spiritual Criminals Identified & Arrested*. Independently Published.

17. I decree that every demonic voice trying to rename, redirect, or confuse my identity is silenced now. I love myself with the voice of God and declare my true identity is rising with power and light. Atunnise, T. (2025). *Spiritual Criminals Identified & Arrested*. Independently Published.

18. Any evil covenant altering my spiritual DNA, be broken now by the blood of Jesus. I command total restoration of who I was created to be before the foundation of the world, in Jesus' mighty name. Atunnise, T. (2025). *Spiritual Criminals Identified & Arrested*. Independently Published.

19. I break free from every counterfeit identity that traps me in wrong paths, relationships, and locations. I declare divine separation from confusion and decree alignment with the truth of who I truly am in Christ. Atunnise, T.

(2025). *Spiritual Criminals Identified & Arrested.* Independently Published.

20. I reject every name, tag, or identity not given to me by God. I decree I shall no longer live in error or confusion. My name shall be honored in the heavens and feared in hell. Atunnise, T. (2025). *Spiritual Criminals Identified & Arrested.* Independently Published.

21. Every satanic mask placed upon me to hide my real self is shattered by the divine fire. I arise in truth and declare my authentic voice, assignment, and nature will shine forth without distortion or delay. Atunnise, T. (2025). *Spiritual Criminals Identified & Arrested.* Independently Published.

22. I decree that the angels of God are now retrieving every stolen spiritual certificate, scroll, and document that defines who I am. I receive divine identity reinstatement and decree unstoppable advancement in my calling. Atunnise, T. (2025). *Spiritual Criminals Identified & Arrested.* Independently Published.

23. In the name of Jesus, I command every demonic imposter using my identity in the spirit realm to be arrested and judged. I walk in spiritual security, boldness, and divine approval from this day forward. Atunnise, T. (2025). *Spiritual Criminals Identified & Arrested.* Independently Published.
24. I decree that the blood of Jesus seals my spiritual fingerprints, image, and voice. No evil force can copy, duplicate, or replace me. I am marked for destiny, and I walk in authority. Atunnise, T. (2025). *Spiritual Criminals Identified & Arrested.* Independently Published.
25. I break the spell of confusion from my mind. I decree mental clarity, divine insight, and supernatural discernment. I shall no longer question who I am or why I exist. My identity is now solid in Christ. Atunnise, T. (2025). *Spiritual Criminals Identified & Arrested.* Independently Published.
26. I decree I shall not live a borrowed life. I cancel every identity switched or programmed

by witchcraft. I reclaim my original throne, crown, and territory, as assigned to me by God, in Jesus' name. Atunnise, T. (2025). *Spiritual Criminals Identified & Arrested*. Independently Published.

27. Every evil mirror reflecting a false version of me is shattered. I decree that only God's version of my identity shall stand. I rise in dominion and walk confidently in my Kingdom assignment without apology. Atunnise, T. (2025). *Spiritual Criminals Identified & Arrested*. Independently Published.

28. In Jesus's name, I release fire against every ancestral altar that manipulated my identity from birth. I break free from generational confusion and reclaim the divine blueprint God originally wrote concerning my life. Atunnise, T. (2025). *Spiritual Criminals Identified & Arrested*. Independently Published.

29. I declare my Spirit, soul, and body are realigned to divine order. I shake off spiritual confusion and declare thatI shall no longer be

found in places I do not belong, and relationships not ordained by God. Atunnise, T. (2025). *Spiritual Criminals Identified & Arrested*. Independently Published.

30. Every demonic transaction done using my image, name, or likeness is revolted now by the blood of Jesus. I decree divine restoration, and I walk in honor, favor, and spiritual accuracy from this moment on. Atunnise, T. (2025). *Spiritual Criminals Identified & Arrested*. Independently Published.

31. I decree that my divine identity is now revealed, respected, and honored in heaven and on earth. I walk in confidence, accuracy, and bonus, and I shall fulfill everything God wrote about me in his word. Atunnise, T. (2025). *Spiritual Criminals Identified & Arrested*. Independently Published.

32. In the name of Jesus, I shut down every demonic surveillance system monitoring my life. Every spiritual camera, mirror, and monitoring eye is shattered by the power of

Jesus' blood. I permanently and completely escaped their network. Atunnise, T. (2025). *Spiritual Criminals Identified & Arrested*. Independently Published.

33. I decree that every astral projection against my household catches Holy Ghost fire. Every evil observer assigned to attack my progress is struck blind and silenced. I walk under divided cover and heavy insulation, now and always. Atunnise, T. (2025). *Spiritual Criminals Identified & Arrested*. Independently Published.

34. Every monitoring spirit, aside from reporting my movements, plans, and next steps, is arrested now by the angels of God. I revoke your assignment and declare confusion in your camp in the mighty name of Jesus Christ. Atunnise, T. (2025). *Spiritual Criminals Identified & Arrested*. Independently Published.

35. I declare that my name, image, and location are erased from every demonic database. My data is inaccessible to evil searchers in the spirit realm. By the power of my divine

authority, I become spiritually invisible to the enemy, effective from today forward. Atunnise, T. (2025). *Spiritual Criminals Identified & Arrested*. Independently Published.

36. I break the power of marine spirits, household enemies, and astral travelers spying on me. Let the fire of the Lord consume their portals of access. From now on, I walk under a supernatural covering that blinds every spiritual enemy. Atunnise, T. (2025). *Spiritual Criminals Identified & Arrested*. Independently Published.

37. I decree by fire every satanic contract written in the Spirit bearing my name is hereby nullified. I invoke the covenant of Jesus's blood to silence and override every demonic agreement holding my life hostage. Atunnise, T. (2025). *Spiritual Criminals Identified & Arrested*. Independently Published.

38. Every soul tie forged through sexual sin, blood packs, or ungodly covenants is broken now. I recover every fragmented part of my

soul and command full restoration of my destiny in the mighty name of Jesus Christ. Atunnise, T. (2025). *Spiritual Criminals Identified & Arrested*. Independently Published.

39. By the authority of the risen Christ, I renounce every ungodly soul connection with people, places, objects, or blurred lies that empower demons. I sever those ties and command divine replacement to be activated in my relationships. Atunnise, T. (2025). *Spiritual Criminals Identified & Arrested*. Independently Published.

40. I speak judgment against ancestral agreements that traded my future for game. Let the fire of God destroy their tokens and seals. I decree freedom from generational packs and release divine inheritance from heaven's storehouse. Atunnise, T. (2025). *Spiritual Criminals Identified & Arrested*. Independently Published.

41. I command every spiritual spiderweb linked to me to destructive relationships to burn now. I am disconnected from every influence

keeping me in bondage. I walk within the new connection God has prepared for my elevation and purpose. Atunnise, T. (2025). *Spiritual Criminals Identified & Arrested*. Independently Published.

42. Let the yoke of every marine, witchcraft, occult, ancestral covenant around my life be shattered now. I decree that the stronghold is broken, and I am released into God's will and divine alignment, permanently, in Jesus' name. Atunnise, T. (2025). *Spiritual Criminals Identified & Arrested*. Independently Published.

43. I decree freedom from emotional soul ties that keep me in cycles of pain and regret. I sever every string of manipulation, guilt, and false attachment. I declare complete soul healing and restoration by the power of God. Atunnise, T. (2025). *Spiritual Criminals Identified & Arrested*. Independently Published.

44. Every generational marriage to spiritual spouses and Demons to ask Sister or covenants, be broken by the covenant power

of Jesus' blood. I divorce every demonic partner and decree restoration of divine marital destiny and spiritual purity. Atunnise, T. (2025). *Spiritual Criminals Identified & Arrested*. Independently Published.

45. In the name of Jesus, I break every generational curse passed down through my bloodline: I decree that the blood of Jesus shatters my cycle of failure, sickness, and limitations, and I step into my divine liberty now. Atunnise, T. (2025). *Spiritual Criminals Identified & Arrested*. Independently Published.

46. I decree that every ancestral altar crying against my destiny is silenced. Forever, by the power of Jesus Christ, I disconnect myself from evil covenants, and I receive a new covenant of blessings, fruitfulness, and forward movement. Atunnise, T. (2025). *Spiritual Criminals Identified & Arrested*. Independently Published.

47. I stand in Christ and decree that my DNA is reprogrammed for success, victory, and divine

acceleration. I reject every evil pattern and command the cycle of backwardness to break permanently by fire, in the name of Jesus. Atunnise, T. (2025). *Spiritual Criminals Identified & Arrested*. Independently Published.

48. I command every familiar Spirit trailing my bloodline to catch fire and be destroyed. I disconnect my soul, body, and Spirit from ancestral grief, sorrow, and tragedy. I declare that my generation is the beginning of a new era of glory. Atunnise, T. (2025). *Spiritual Criminals Identified & Arrested*. Independently Published.

49. Every generational curse that causes marital delay, disappointment, or heartbreak is broken. I declare that my love story, marriage, and relationships are now established and fulfilled. I declare righteous peace and divine harmony in the name of Jesus. Atunnise, T. (2025). *Spiritual Criminals Identified & Arrested*. Independently Published.

50. I release the fire of the Holy Ghost against every ancestral curse manifesting as poverty. I decree that financial freedom, divine ideas, and supernatural provision are my portion. I declare the curse of financial struggle is ended in Jesus' name! Atunnise, T. (2025). *Spiritual Criminals Identified & Arrested*. Independently Published.

IN MY FATHER'S HANDS 2

IN MY FATHER'S HANDS 2

IN MY FATHER'S HANDS 2

IN MY FATHER'S HANDS 2

IN MY FATHER'S HANDS 2

IN MY FATHER'S HANDS 2

www.ingramcontent.com/pod-product-compliance
Lightning Source LLC
Chambersburg PA
CBHW050652160426
43194CB00010B/1908